Philosophical Summary

The Subtle Act of Not Giving a F*ck

Mason Madison (Author)

ISBN: 978-1-387-48536-9

Contents

Mason Madison

*The Subtle Act of Not Giving a F*ck*

Philosophical Summary

CHAPTER I

Don't Try

"After all, no truly happy person feels the need to stand in front of a mirror and recite that she's happy. She just is."

Manson begins the book by bemoaning modern culture's unreasonable demands. Many people's lives are consumed by the pursuit of the "American Dream." Be the best in every way: richer, more handsome, leaner, funnier, happier, more admired, and so on. It just goes on and on. This is standard self-help advice, and it all focuses on one thing: what you lack. Your flaws, or how you perceive them. When we only think on what could be better in our life, it acts as a constant reminder of how far we have fallen.

A big house, a nice automobile, and a big TV are widely touted as signs of a prosperous life. Daily advertising claim that getting more, more, more is the key to happiness. They pay special attention to your apparent flaws. Giving a crap about these concerns is good for business, but not for one's personal health. It's harmful for your mental health to follow after these fragile ideals and things since they only satisfy you for a short period of time while you wait for the next shiny product to be rammed down your throat. The key to living a successful life is to worry less and focus on what is genuinely essential.

Nowadays, owing to social media, you can always see 100 of your pals having a good time, even if you're having a bad day. Then it's tough not to ponder if something is wrong with your life, if something is missing, or if your troubles are merely the product of character faults. In contrast, if someone had a horrible day 50 years ago, they would have probably acknowledged it and gone about their business. If you glance at Facebook today, your already bad day will get even worse, and your life will feel even more bleak. You feel horrible right now, and then you feel bad because of your poor feelings. It's unhealthy, and Manson refers to it as the "feedback cycle from hell." When we only see people's happy moments, we begin to assume that we, too, are entitled to them on a regular basis. Manson criticizes typical self-help advice that advocates continuously chasing the wonderful things in life, arguing that doing so is actually a terrible experience. Accepting a terrible experience, on the other hand, can be a beneficial one. While this may appear to be confusing, it can be explained as follows: You feel less valuable while you work toward a goal. For example, continually attempting to be perceived as cool and popular (positive) will make you self-conscious and almost certainly cause you to feel some self-loathing (negative). While pursuing the negative, such as starting a business because you enjoy the process and don't mind the crazy amount of effort necessary (negative), you will have a much better chance of producing a successful, profitable firm than someone who begins a business solely to make money (positive). Suffering involves the desire to avoid conflict. Manson then offers us three rules to abide by in our quest to give less fucks in the proper way:

- Being comfortable with one's differences does not imply indifference. Being unconcerned with what other people think in the first place, as well as lacking the courage to express an opinion, are common causes of indifference, which is lame and cowardly. Instead, it means acting in accordance with your carefully chosen values and beliefs, regardless of the challenges you may face along the way..
- To be unconcerned with difficulty, you must be preoccupied with something more essential. It is also

crucial to have substantial and meaningful things going on in your life; otherwise, you will get too obsessed with the insignificant and unimportant. The mind craves stimulus, so why not make it worthwhile?

- You are constantly making decisions about what matters, whether you realize it or not. It is up to you to recognize this and decide whether your current fucks are benefiting or harming you.

This isn't to say you should be apathetic; rather, make informed decisions about your values and stick to them. Make a deliberate decision about what you care about. It's okay to admit that you may not be able to solve the world's problems, such as global warming or cancer, or achieve the lofty goals you set for yourself as a child. Many people come to the obvious and simple conclusion that family, closest friends, and pizza are among the few things that truly deserve our "most fucks." And, believe it or not, this is plenty.

KEY LESSONS

- Don't buy into the idea that you aren't enough or that you don't have enough in the current culture.

- Social media doesn't reflect reality and only serves to reinforce the feedback loop from hell.

- The desire for a good experience is actually a bad one. Accepting a bad experience, however, is in reality a good experience.

- Don't be indifferent when deciding to give less fucks; instead, embrace your uniqueness.
- You must care about something other than the adversity in order to not care about it.

- You are constantly choosing what to care about.

CHAPTER II

Happiness Is a Problem

"Problems never stop;

they merely get exchanged and/or upgraded."

The way to happiness is not to avoid pain. Actually, suffering is an essential part of our development and biology; it serves as a catalyst for transformation. Suffering, both physical and mental, inspires us to act and focuses our attention on what is most essential. Although we may despise it, it is undeniably valuable and should be utilized. In some clear situations, such as when we were youngsters and touched a hot stove, pain can be utilized to teach us valuable lessons. We rapidly learn not to do that again. On the other side, avoiding emotional pain may lead to a sheltered life. Rejection after chasing your crush might generate fear of failure, making it difficult to pursue your actual objectives in the future in order to prevent the brief emotional agony you experienced previously. Living in such a remote, comfortable culture that avoids life's unavoidable annoyances can keep us from experiencing a healthy amount of misery.

Instead than attempting to live a life free of troubles, seek to have excellent problems. Problems in life, no matter who you are, never go away; they either change or worsen. Resolving these concerns leads to happiness. What distinguishes it is that it is a never-ending work in progress. The idea is to choose challenges that you enjoy tackling. We create the framework for better problems tomorrow by fixing current concerns today. Denial is your adversary, so be honest with yourself and recognize the difficulties you need to confront. Some people choose to tell themselves that there is nothing they can do to fix their difficulties, yet this strategy has no benefits. We can receive a brief high from blaming and denying, but long-term contentment comes from enduring through any discomfort brought on by an issue.

Emotions do not always accurately reflect reality. While emotions should not be treated as gospel, they might point us in the correct way. You should question them on a regular basis. Suppressing negative emotions is a prevalent practice in many cultures, particularly in the present self-help market. Ignoring these sensations will not make them go away, and doing so may result in long-term consequences. Face them and remember that pain has a purpose. On the other hand, rationalizing every behavior by blaming your feelings is neither mature nor useful. Because emotions fluctuate, pursuing goals exclusively based on emotion is doomed to fail. As Manson so eloquently puts it, "Who lives their entire life based on their emotions? children aged under three breeds of dogs What else do dogs and three-year-old children do? Poop is on the carpet." It's reassuring to believe that getting the perfect career, spouse, car, etc. can lead to ultimate bliss. Even the ideal job can bring stress, and you'll wind up having to fix the dream car you bought. It is impossible to be content and happy all of the time. Nobody has it, but everyone wishes they did.

Many people ask themselves, "What would make me happy?" when deciding what they want out of life. Instead, ask yourself, "What am I willing to fight for?" Many people desire to start a business, become entrepreneurs, and make a lot of money. Few people are willing to take the risk of abandoning their jobs and working 70-hour workweeks to start a business, knowing that it may fail and be worthless. Although some beliefs may appeal to you, in order to excel at anything, you must be invested in both the process and the end result. You can't only want the benefit and skip the effort. Consider carefully what you are willing to battle for in order to be happy. In reality, there is no obvious end in sight. After you've overcome and resolved your initial problems, you'll progress to the next round of tasks, which should be better and more advanced. You shouldn't want it to end because it never does. As the saying goes, the joy is in the journey, not the destination.

KEY LESSONS

- Don't always try to avoid suffering and pain; they can be a teacher and be helpful.
- Strive for a life with good problems, not a life without them.
- Blame and denial can make us feel better right away, but enduring the pain a problem causes and sticking with it makes us happy in the long run.
- Emotions should be questioned because they aren't always accurate.
- It is impossible to consistently feel content and joyful.
- What are you willing to endure suffering for? is a better question to ask yourself than what will make you happy.

CHAPTER III

You Are Not Special

"We're not all exceptional. It turns out that merely feeling good about yourself doesn't really mean anything unless you have a good reason to feel good about yourself."

At the beginning of the chapter, Manson gives opposing perspectives on the 1980s self-esteem movement. He claims that when the concept of having a high sense of oneself gained widespread, many people grew entitled. You need a reason to be proud of yourself; simply being proud of yourself will not get you anywhere. People who continually feel good about themselves regardless of their circumstances do not become outstanding; rather, they become entitled and delusional. When your entire attention is focused on how amazing you feel, it is easier to mislead yourself into believing you are achieving great things. Your feelings regarding the negative aspects of your life should be a better reflection of your self-worth. Are you able to be absolutely honest with yourself and focus on the areas in which you need to improve? Feeling good all of the time is meaningless if your life is falling apart around you. This sense of entitlement can lead to delusory self-confidence. Because of the need to feel good all the time, being preoccupied and self-absorbed on feeling good will eventually come at the price of others. As Manson so eloquently puts it, "after all, it takes a lot of energy and labor to convince yourself that your shit doesn't stink, especially when you've actually been living in a toilet."

On the other hand, believing that your issues are constantly exceptional, singular, and insurmountable is also a form of entitlement. It takes just as much effort and self-delusion to frame every problem as a victimization of you as it does to think you have no problems at all. One of these two ways is how entitlement manifests itself:

8

- I'm the best, and the rest of you are garbage, so I should get special treatment.

- Since I'm terrible and the rest of you are awesome, I should get special treatment. Whatever your issue, it's likely that millions of other people have faced it before you. This does not imply that it is not painful or challenging. Simply put, neither it nor your circumstances are unique. The first step toward resolving your circumstances is frequently realizing that they aren't unique.

We are average in the great bulk of our daily activities. Even if you actually excel in one area, your performance in the majority of others is most likely ordinary. That is to be expected because perfecting anything takes a lot of time and dedication, therefore it is acceptable to expect that. Although the bulk of us are rather typical, only the extremes in life receive the most attention. In today's media, which includes TV, YouTube, and Facebook, to mention a few, only the exceptional or completely bizarre make the cut. At the very top, 99.9 percentile. The utmost worst and ultimate greatest. The profusion of information leads us to believe that the extraordinary is the usual and that we live ordinary, mundane lives. That is not the case. The majority of life is mundane and routine. Overstimulation in the media fosters vulnerabilities, which inspire entitlement and attempts to compensate through addiction.

At a time when the current standard of success is becoming "exceptional," it can be tough to hear that the key to emotional wellness is to accept that most of life will be prosaic and unremarkable. This isn't to suggest you shouldn't aim to be your best self, but if your happiness is dependent on achieving society's definition of extraordinary, you're unlikely to succeed. You'll feel inadequate, or worse, you'll sacrifice your morals or step on others to do this.

Accepting this new way of thinking may be difficult at first. You'll feel a lot better when you do this. As you let go of the pressure to be the perfect human being, you'll begin to appreciate the little things. hooking up with an old acquaintance, creating something out of nothing, or helping a neighbor These things may appear to be commonplace. They are, but in life, what matters most is the ordinary.

KEY LESSONS

- Be sincere with yourself and put your attention on solving your problems and achieving your goals rather than just feeling good for no apparent reason.
- Your issues are neither unique nor exceptional.
- Recognize that most of life is ordinary and that the media often portrays unrealistic situations.
- Life's true significance lies in the everyday.

CHAPTER IV

The Value of Suffering

"Everything we think and feel about a situation ultimately comes back to how valuable we perceive it to be."

Manson begins the chapter by telling the story of the famed Japanese soldier Second Lieutenant Hiroo Onoda. When he was sent to fight in the jungles of the Philippines in 1944, he was given the order to stand and fight no matter what, never giving up. Even after the war ended in 1945, Onada refused to acknowledge that the Japanese had surrendered. Despite the fact that the Americans had dropped leaflets across the jungle declaring the end of the war, Onoda mistook this for a ploy and continued to hide, periodically terrifying the natives he came across, until he was ultimately located in 1972, nearly 30 years after the war had finished. Even though he was suffering and fighting for a defunct kingdom, he really believed in his cause. Instead than considering how to escape suffering, evaluate whether your suffering is truly necessary. When Onada returned to Japan, he realized that his suffering had been in vain. He got sad and relocated to Brazil, where he lived out his days until his death. Self-awareness is multi-layered:

- Layer 1: Simply put, this just tries to comprehend how you feel. "I'm happy,"

- Layer 2: is the capacity to ponder why you are feeling the way you are. Although it is more difficult to understand this layer, finding the cause is crucial. Planning for a change can begin once the root cause has been identified.

- Layer 3: The most valuable and hardest to obtain is this. personal principles. "In what way are you choosing to evaluate yourself?" "By what standards do you judge success and failure?"

Given that these values govern all we do, it is critical to define them positively. If the definition of success or failure is not chosen carefully, everything else will be out of step. Your daily feelings, fears, motivation, and focus will all suffer if your values are not carefully analyzed and followed. Finally, how we feel and think about a situation is determined by the value we attribute to it. The way you perceive your circumstance, how you choose to measure it, and how you value it is more important than what is absolutely true about it. While issues are unavoidable, not all problems are the same. We have power over what our difficulties imply depending on how we interpret them and the yardstick we use to assess them.

If they are not controlled or moderated, certain common values can quickly cause issues for people. To name a few:

- Pleasure. While some pleasures are great in moderation, prioritizing your life around them can often be disastrous. Drug addicts seek pleasure, and morbidly obese people seek the transient gratification that unhealthy food offers. Living a healthy, happy life is not either. Marketing campaigns constantly push pleasure down our throats in an effort to dull and detach us from reality. Put your priorities and values in order, and pleasure will come as a natural byproduct.

- material gain. Putting too much emphasis on "keeping up with the Joneses" can be harmful to your mental health. You are likely to lack psychologically healthy values like honesty and compassion if you gauge your worth by the accumulation of expensive possessions and status symbols. It's highly likely that you're an asshole as well.

- Constantly being right. Your development will be hampered if you are unable to empathize with others and learn from new perspectives.

- Remaining optimistic. This doesn't mean you shouldn't make an effort to be upbeat most of the time. It's better to let it out when life deals you a particularly nasty hand. Instead of addressing the problem, repressing these negative feelings simply delays it.

Over time, running a 10k makes us happier than Netflix binges. Instead of playing video games, we'd rather spend our evenings starting a small business. Even though they are difficult and painful, when we reflect on them later, it is these successes that bring us happiness. Enjoyment and success will follow if you ingrain some positive values. In order to choose the right values:

Good values — a) reality-based b) socially constructive c) Immediate and controllable

Bad values — a) superstitious b) socially destructive c) Not immediate or controllable

Honesty, openness, respect for oneself, originality, modesty, creativity, work ethic, curiosity, and self-defense are a few examples of good values.

Being popular with everyone, gaining power through coercion or violence, becoming wealthy for status alone, and being with others are a few examples of bad values.

Set higher values—the things you care about—as your top priorities. Better problems will result from this. Better life will result from this.

KEY LESSONS

- Ask yourself if you are suffering for worthwhile reasons rather than trying to avoid it.
- Give careful consideration to the values you decide to uphold.
- The value we assign to a situation determines how we feel and think about it in every way.
- Good values — a) reality-based b) socially constructive c) Immediate and controllable
- Bad values — a) superstitious b) socially destructive c) Not immediate or controllable

CHAPTER V

You Are Always Choosing

"We don't always control what happens to us. But we always control how we interpret what happens to us, as well as how we respond."

The level of control we feel over our circumstances impacts whether they are painful or joyful. When a situation is thrust upon us, we may feel miserable and mistreated because we believe we have no control over it. In contrast to those, we feel driven and powerful when we opt to address our own difficulties. As an example, Manson offers the situation of being compelled to run a marathon under fear of force and electing to accept the challenge by committing to training ahead of time and crossing the finish line in front of friends and family. Same distance, same hardship, but different points of view on the matter.

Manson then tells the story of William James. William had a difficult existence his entire life. He was a social outcast because of a multitude of potentially fatal health issues, and he seemed to fail at everything he tried. He took the decision to engage in his own experiment while depressed and contemplating suicide. For a year, he would believe he had no excuses and was solely responsible for everything that had ever occurred to him. As you may expect, he drastically transformed his life and is now renowned as the father of American Phycology. He attributed all of his life's triumphs to this mindset shift. We cannot always control what occurs to us, but we can always choose how we interpret events and how we respond to them. We already interpret the significance of every incident in our life, whether we intend to or not. It is up to us to decide how we interpret things based on the values and guiding principles we choose to live by. These are all measurements. It all boils down to carefully choosing what we care about. Who or what do we choose to care for, and what ideals guide our actions? Do these choices reflect your values?

The more accountability we accept in life, the more power we have. Fault and responsibility are distinct notions; we are regularly held liable for things that were not our fault. While accepting responsibility for our accomplishments is straightforward, accepting responsibility for our failures is significantly more important. Situations like these result in learning and development. You only injure yourself when you blame others.

The game of poker is the second example Manson offers to demonstrate how, while luck is always there, it does not dictate the long-term outcomes of the game. This can be used as a guide for daily life. We are all dealt cards, some of which are superior to others. It's easy to feel unfairly treated by the cards given to you, but how you choose to play them is ultimately what matters. choices you make, risks you chose to take, and consequences you choose to accept Those that thrive in life find a way to maximize their possibilities regardless of their circumstances.

It makes no difference whether you have suffered unjust financial, physical, or emotional pain. Even if it wasn't your fault, you always have control over how you react. You are always in control, whether you choose to pout and feel sorry for yourself or to move forward and make the best decisions you can.

KEY LESSONS

- Depending on the level of control we feel we have over a problem, it can either be painful or enjoyable.
- We have more control over life the more responsibility we take on.
- No matter the situation they are dealt, those who succeed in life make the most of it.
- You are always in charge of how you react.

CHAPTER VI

You're Wrong About Everything (But So Am I)

"Certainty is the enemy of growth"

Manson believes that progress is a never-ending process in which we only ever become slightly less incorrect rather than progressing from one erroneous direction to another. Rather of pursuing life's ultimate "rights," we should attempt to right the wrongs in our lives so that we are a bit less wrong in the future. This technique is, in fact, extremely scientific. Our acts function as experiments, and our values function as hypotheses. The feelings and reactions that result are our data.

Self-imposed constraints, such as the belief that we are not attractive enough, give us temporary comfort in the present by driving us to expect greater achievement and happiness in the future. These ideas do not serve us in the long run, but we continue to hold onto them because we believe they are true. We believe that if we behave in a specific way, we will always know how the story will finish. Certainty stifles growth. Instead of pursuing confidence in our actions, we should seek doubt. In any event, nothing is certain until it happens. You will grow when you have doubts about your own convictions. You will not act to shape the future if you have doubts about it. The easiest approach to change and progress is to focus on our flaws and mistakes. Your views are mainly false; some are more false than others. The human mind is both immensely brilliant and imperfect. Recognizing this might be rather unsettling, but it is critical.

We are continually urged by conventional wisdom to "trust your instincts" or to use our initiative. Given how often we make errors, this is not necessarily sound counsel. A more rational course of action would be to question our aims and motives more. We are erasing the wrongs in our lives and ensuring that we are a little less wrong tomorrow by questioning our assumptions and practicing persistent self-skepticism.

Manson's next narrative is about Erin, a lady he met at a self-improvement conference. Erin believes she can stop death, but she also believes she must be in a relationship with Manson in order to do it. She is essentially a paranoid stalker. Manson goes on to say that she is a compulsive self-improvement shopper, spending thousands of dollars on seminars, conferences, and publications. The most ludicrous feature of this circumstance is Erin's strict adherence to all of the instructions and lessons. She has a dream, is tenacious, employs visualization, and perseveres in the face of adversity. What is the problem? Because of her weak moral standards, nothing counts. Because of her certainty, she is unable to see beyond this ludicrous conviction.

Any degree of assurance is illusory, and it typically produces insecurity. You may check your partner's phone for texts, but this rarely ends there. You might then be concerned about a second phone, Facebook messages, and so on. According to Manson, the more you strive to be certain about anything, the more uncertain and insecure you will feel, as the backwards rule is once again at work. Fortunately, the contrary is also true: embracing doubt and ignorance will make you feel more at comfortable knowing what you don't know. Uncertainty liberates us from self-judgment and allows us to experience without bias or constraint. Uncertainty promotes growth and provides us with many more opportunities to learn new abilities. Uncertainty allows us to be honest with ourselves and recognize that changing our actions and beliefs that we have been using to handle our challenges is the only way to address them effectively. It helps us make better decisions by making us question our present ideals.

The following statement from Manson describes a notion he coined as "Manson's Law of Avoidance."

The more something threatens your identity, the more you will avoid it.

He goes on to suggest that if something threatens your perception of how successful or unsuccessful you are, you will avoid it. When most people understand their place in the world, they act as they would like others to perceive them to act. If you're the "nice guy," you'll always be polite and avoid any potential disputes. Even though changing this comfort could improve your life, it is disconcerting. If you internalize these attributes and ideals, your life perspective may become very limited. We can't change until we can change how we see ourselves. Instead than following the traditional advice to "discover yourself," never know who you are. This will motivate you to keep learning and growing while also accepting new possibilities and realizing your own potential.

Manson suggests identifying yourself in the most plain and ordinary way possible. Avoid being one-of-a-kind or extraordinary. Do not regard yourself as a failure or a victim. Consider yourself a buddy, a collaborator, or a creator. This may require letting go of a flawless future self-image you have and the entitlement that generally comes with it, but you will feel so much better and freer on the other side. To cultivate a little uncertainty in your life, Manson proposes asking yourself three questions. It is challenging to learn to question our own views.

- What if I'm mistaken?
- What would it mean if I was mistaken?
- Would being incorrect lead to a better or worse issue than my current issue, for both myself and others?

KEY LESSONS

- Never do we go from wrong to right; rather, we always go from wrong to slightly less wrong.
- By putting our faith in future success and happiness, self-imposed limiting beliefs provide us with momentary solace in the here and now.
- Long-term benefits of these beliefs are negligible, but we continue to hold onto them because we believe they are true.
- Challenge your current viewpoints and the reasons for them.
- Your tendency to avoid something increases as it poses a threat to your identity.
- Rather than taking the conventional advice to "find yourself," never know who you are.
- Simplest ways to describe who you are.

CHAPTER VII

Failure Is The Way Forward

"We can be truly successful only at something
we're willing to fail at. If we're unwilling to fail,
then we're unwilling to succeed."

Repeated failure leads to improvement in anything. The most typical reason someone is better than you at something is that they have failed more frequently than you. We only learn to avoid failure as we become older. A child would never give up on learning to walk just because it "isn't something they're excellent at." We don't reach our full potential because we try to prevent failure by doing only what we're sure about. We are incapable of succeeding because we are incapable of failing. This could happen as a result of hanging onto damaging values. As indicated in Chapter 4, having process-oriented values will aid with this. It is far preferable to adopt a value such as "Always have fun while being courteous of others" over "Always act in a way that everyone likes me." The latter is beyond our control and, if implemented, will almost certainly fail and cause distress. The first value is process-oriented, necessitating continuous improvement with each contact. It is a lifelong project that will never be completed.

Typically, our greatest success emerges from our greatest adversity. We can often use pain to our advantage. Discomfort should be encouraged in some situations rather than avoided. Pushing over the pump's pain threshold is critical for progressing in the gym. In order to evolve psychologically, it is frequently required to go through some form of emotional agony. Pain can be a catalyst for change. Only when we are in agony do we feel compelled to change our current circumstances or morals. Chasing a high to alleviate the pain of a low is simply a temporary fix. The need to feel better as soon as possible leads us astray, leading us to believe that everything is OK the way it is.

Learn how to deal with the pain you've chosen. Accept and enjoy your pain. Act nonetheless.

You must take action. Action is the cause of motivation as well as one of its effects. In general, people think:

Emotional inspiration → Motivation → Desirable action

It's simple to believe you have no chance of success if you don't feel particularly motivated to take action toward something you want to achieve. Fortunately, motivation is an endless cycle that is not limited to the three chains mentioned above:

Inspiration Motivation → Action → Inspiration → Motivation → Action → Etc.

Motivating yourself will come from action. Knowing this, you can now do the following:

Action → Inspiration → Motivation

If you lack motivation in any area of your life, simply take action. The motivation will arrive later. If the scale of an issue or project is prompting you to put it off, start small. Simply force yourself to begin, no matter how small or trivial. Maintaining momentum and establishing a flow state become considerably easier once you get started. Failure becomes immaterial and overcoming procrastination becomes simpler with a "just do something" mindset. This concept can be used to any scenario in your life, such as a work assignment or a relationship problem. Simply take action. It is always possible to act; inspiration and drive will follow.

KEY LESSONS

- The majority of the time, if someone is better than you at something, it's because they have experienced more failures than you have.
- You can't be willing to succeed if you're also unwilling to fail.
- Choose values that are focused on processes.
- Action is both the cause and the result of motivation.
- Adopt the "just do something" philosophy.

CHAPTER VIII

The Importance of Saying No

"We are defined by what we choose to reject. And if we reject nothing, we essentially have no identity at all."

Although freedom provides the prospect of greater meaning, it cannot provide greater meaning in and of itself. Meaning is produced by a limiting of commitments and beliefs. Self-help literature and popular culture now teach us to be accepting of everyone and everything. We must be able to reject certain things or we will be left with nothing to stand for. Following the crowd leads to a life devoid of values that is ultimately meaningless. Avoiding rejection can lead to a life without direction, which is easier in the short term because we don't feel the initial agony. Long-term commitment is essential for truly meaningful things in life, and we can only make that commitment if we break previous ones. We can't commit to our beliefs if we don't rule out alternatives.

To value anything, we must first care about it. In order to value X, we must reject non-X. What we choose to reject is what defines us. According to Manson, demonstrating entitlement takes the form of avoiding rejection. The entitled expect to always feel good by not upsetting themselves or others, and they are willing to go to any length to escape rejection. This is a meaningless existence motivated solely by pleasure and selfishness. It is critical to learn how to handle rejection in your life. You should be able to

26

communicate your actual feelings or leave a job you dislike without fear of repercussions. We can all agree that honesty is a virtue to strive for in our lives, but it limits our ability to say no to things we don't want to do.

In life, we require boundaries. There are unhealthy and healthy forms of love, according to Manson. When two people use their feelings for one another as a means of escaping their problems, unhealthy love develops. When two people support one another while resolving their own issues, healthy love is formed. According to Manson, the distinction is due to two factors:

- How well each person takes accountability
- The capacity of each partner to reject and be rejected by the other.

A common feature of unhealthy relationships is an inability to give or receive rejection. This is simply another example of arrogance and a refusal to accept responsibility for problems. A healthy relationship entails each person solving their own difficulties in order to feel good about the other, as opposed to trying to feel good about the other by fixing one other's problems or avoiding problems altogether. Manson's final statement on the matter is as follows: "Giving a fuck about your spouse means doing so regardless of the fucks he or she gives, not giving a fuck about everything they give a fuck about. That is pure love, my little one."

KEY LESSONS

- Meaning develops as beliefs and commitments become more focused.
- What we choose to reject defines who we are.
- Rejection is a valuable skill to have.
- When two people use their feelings for one another as a means of escaping their problems, it results in unhealthy love.

- Healthy love occurs when two people support one another while resolving their individual issues.

CHAPTER IX

Freedom Through Commitment

"Yes, breadth of experience is likely necessary and desirable when you're young—after all, you have to go out there and discover what seems worth investing yourself in. But depth is where the gold is buried. And you have to stay committed to something and go deep to dig it up. That's true in relationships, in a career, in building a great lifestyle—in everything."

Through sophisticated marketing and commercial culture, we are given the notion that more is always better. In a nutshell, have more stuff and earn more money. Manson thinks the contrary is true, using the rationale for what psychologists call the paradox of choice. This occurs when we have an abundance of options and opportunities to choose from, making it difficult to be entirely content with the decision we make since we are constantly aware of the opportunities we missed. The drive to ensure that you make the best decision in the pursuit of perfection can lead to tension and worry. Many people may experience "paralysis by analysis," which occurs when they become so overwhelmed with the possibilities that they are unable to make a decision at all.

Manson says that, while focusing on a tiny percentage of life's experiences may prohibit us from experiencing as many as we'd want, doing so is important in order to reap the benefits of experience's richness. Going the quantity way results in lower returns. The first place you travel outside of your native nation will provide a variety of new viewpoints and experiences, but the benefits will be drastically lessened by the time you visit your thirty-first new country. The fiftyth is much less. This applies to every superficial choice that people make, such as material goods, hobbies, occupations, sexual partners, and so on.

According to Manson, the ability to open himself up to commitment has been a significant growth for him in recent years. Reject everyone and everything except the best people, experiences, and values in your life. Contrary to conventional thinking, dedication can lead to emancipation and freedom. By focusing your attention on fewer, more important items, you can decrease unimportant distractions. A more focused effort will almost always result in improvements in your chosen undertakings.

KEY LESSONS

- The gold is buried in the depths.
- Make yourself available to commitment.
- Discard all but the best.

CHAPTER X

...And Then You Die

"Without acknowledging the ever-present gaze of death, the superficial will appear important, and the important will appear superficial."

Because it is so frightening, most people avoid talking or even thinking about death. Manson believes that thinking about it more regularly is vital since death gives life meaning. Without it, everything seems small and senseless, and values are meaningless.

We can learn two key lessons from Ernest Becker's Pulitzer Prize–winning book The Denial of Death, according to Manson:

- Humans are exceptional because we are the only species that can conceptualize and think about oneself in an abstract way. Considering the recent past and the distant future, imagining hypothetical scenarios, imagining potential alternative outcomes to events and situations, etc. We are the only species capable of imagining a world without us and the certainty of our own demise as a result of this ability. According to Becker, this results in "death terror," a profound existential anxiety that underlies everything we think or do.

- Becker asserts that each of us has a dual personality. the conceptual self, which includes our identity and how we see ourselves. The fact that we all know we will eventually die physically terrifies us so much that we attempt to create a conceptual self that will live forever. Our dream is to leave a conceptual legacy that will last much longer

31

than our physical self through our offspring, accomplishments, influence, and legacy. These initiatives, which Becker refers to as "immortality projects," give meaning to our lives and fulfill our innate desire to never truly die.

Our ideals are our ambitions for eternal life. This can generate problems because far too many individuals attempt to impose their conceptual self on the outside world rather than confronting the reality of death. They strive for success and power for no other purpose than to assure the endurance of their name. Even though it is terrible, death is unavoidable. We can choose our immortality projects (values) more freely and wisely when we are fully at ease with this.

The Stoics of Ancient Greece and Rome laid the groundwork for us to confront our mortality on a regular basis. They learned that constantly thinking about death makes you appreciate life and the simple things in it more. Buddhist meditation techniques can help you prepare for death. The goal is to transcend the ego and reach enlightened bliss while still living.

This exercise is critical because it exposes the shallow, flimsy, and weak ideals that we may be acting on right now. Death causes us to consider the more important and challenging question: What will be your legacy? Rather of squandering time attempting to garner a bit more attention, a few new followers, or constantly surfing the internet for junk you don't need.

According to Becker, this is the only question in life. We avoid it because it is tough and terrifying, and none of us are sure what we are doing. Avoidance encourages unproductive values to infiltrate our minds and take over our desires and objectives. Consider this instead:

Will the world be a better place once you're gone?

Will you make a difference to anything or anyone?

Because death is the one certainty in life, it must act as a guide for our decisions and moral standards. It is vital to choose ideals that go beyond self-serving in order to be at peace with death. be concerned with something larger than oneself A total inward attention leads to entitlement and the belief that greatness is deserved rather than gained. This mode of thinking is appealing because it causes us to believe that we are constantly subjected to personal injustices, yet it is lethal to our spirits. The fact that, despite living in a culture that prioritizes material abundance, psychological pain is at an all-time high demonstrates this. People are abdicating their obligations and relying on society to meet all of their demands. This inflated sense of illusory superiority is what motivates people to procrastinate and delay taking action, making them scared to try because they are terrified of failing. The terms "great success" and "great attention" are commonly used interchangeably.

You will only die because you were fortunate enough to have a life to begin with. Keep reminding yourself, whether through reading, meditation, or some other wild activity that makes your heart race. Manson concludes: "Everything has become easier as a result of his acceptance of my death and realization of my own frailty, such as untangling my addictions, recognizing and confronting my entitlement, taking ownership of my issues, enduring my fears and uncertainties, accepting my failures, and embracing rejections. The more I stare into the darkness, the calmer the world becomes, the brighter life becomes, and I have less unconscious resistance to, well, anything."

KEY LESSONS

- Life has meaning because of death.
- We can choose our immortality projects, or values, more freely and intelligently if we can accept death.
- Being constantly aware of death makes you more appreciative of life and the little things in it.

- You are only going to pass away because you were fortunate enough to have lived.

Conclusion

You now understand the strategy for developing fewer fucks as well as a number of other useful principles. I like to go over each chapter's KEY LESSONS once a week to ensure that the lessons are remembered. This is something I practice for this book and all of the others I've written to guarantee that the major principles are truly ingrained in my mind and fast become habits and reactions in my daily life.

Thank you for your interest in my book. I hope you found this to be beneficial and enjoyable. But before you depart, I have one small request...

If you have a minute, with LOVE, please write a REVIEW on this book.

THE END

CPSIA information can be obtained
at www.ICGtesting.com
Printed in the USA
LVHW080205100123
736835LV00016B/1142

9 781387 485369